797,885 Books

are available to read at

www.ForgottenBooks.com

Forgotten Books' App
Available for mobile, tablet & eReader

ISBN 978-1-332-16810-1
PIBN 10293033

This book is a reproduction of an important historical work. Forgotten Books uses
state-of-the-art technology to digitally reconstruct the work, preserving the original format
whilst repairing imperfections present in the aged copy. In rare cases, an imperfection in
the original, such as a blemish or missing page, may be replicated in our edition. We do,
however, repair the vast majority of imperfections successfully; any imperfections that
remain are intentionally left to preserve the state of such historical works.

Forgotten Books is a registered trademark of FB &c Ltd.
Copyright © 2017 FB &c Ltd.
FB &c Ltd, Dalton House, 60 Windsor Avenue, London, SW19 2RR.
Company number 08720141. Registered in England and Wales.

For support please visit www.forgottenbooks.com

1 MONTH OF
FREE
READING

at

www.ForgottenBooks.com

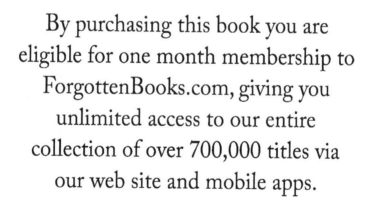

By purchasing this book you are
eligible for one month membership to
ForgottenBooks.com, giving you
unlimited access to our entire
collection of over 700,000 titles via
our web site and mobile apps.

To claim your free month visit:
www.forgottenbooks.com/free293033

* Offer is valid for 45 days from date of purchase. Terms and conditions apply.

English
Français
Deutsche
Italiano
Español
Português

www.forgottenbooks.com

Mythology Photography **Fiction**
Fishing Christianity **Art** Cooking
Essays Buddhism Freemasonry
Medicine **Biology** Music **Ancient**
Egypt Evolution Carpentry Physics
Dance Geology **Mathematics** Fitness
Shakespeare **Folklore** Yoga Marketing
Confidence Immortality Biographies
Poetry **Psychology** Witchcraft
Electronics Chemistry History **Law**
Accounting **Philosophy** Anthropology
Alchemy Drama Quantum Mechanics
Atheism Sexual Health **Ancient History**
Entrepreneurship Languages Sport
Paleontology Needlework Islam
Metaphysics Investment Archaeology
Parenting Statistics Criminology
Motivational

STATE OF NEVADA

☙ THE NEVADA IRRIGATION DISTRICT ACT

Pamphlet No. 9

ISSUED BY

J. G. SCRUGHAM, State Engineer

CARSON CITY, NEVADA

STATE PRINTING OFFICE : : : JOE FARNSWORTH, SUPERINTENDENT

1920

THE NEVADA IRRIGATION DISTRICT ACT

Stats. 1919, page 84

CHAP. 64—*An Act to provide for the organization and government of irrigation districts, for the irrigation and drainage of lands and other related undertakings thereby, and for the acquisition and distribution of water and other property, construction, operation and maintenance of works, diversion, storage, distribution, collection, and carriage of water, cooperation with the United States; and matters properly connected therewith.*

[Approved March 19, 1919]

SECTION 1. A majority in number of the holders of title, or evidence of title, to lands susceptible of one mode of irrigation from a common source or combined sources, and by the same system or combined systems of works, may propose the organization of an irrigation district under this act; *provided*, said holders of title or evidence of title shall hold such title or evidence of title to at least one-half part of the total area of the land in the proposed district; *provided, further*, that every signer of a petition for the organization of an irrigation district shall be the holder of title or evidence of title to at least five acres of land within the proposed district. The equalized county assessment roll next preceding the presentation of a petition for the organization of an irrigation district shall be sufficient evidence of title for the purpose of this act, but other evidence may be received, including receipts or other evidence of rights of entrymen on land under any law of the United States, and such entrymen shall be competent signers of such petition, and the land on which they have made entries shall, for the purpose of said petition, be considered as owned by them. Such entrymen shall share all the privileges and obligations of freeholders and owners of private land within the district, under the several provisions of this act, including the right to vote and hold office, subject to the terms of the act of Congress entitled "An act to promote reclamation of arid lands," approved August 11, 1916. The petitioners may determine in said petition whether the proposed district shall be divided into three, five, or seven divisions, and whether it shall have three, five, or seven directors, but if no number is named in the petition the board of county commissioners may determine whether the number shall be three, five, or seven.

SEC. 2. Whenever it is proposed to organize an irrigation district a petition shall first be presented to the board of county commissioners of the county in which the lands or the greater portion thereof are situated, signed by the required number, possessing the qualifications provided for in section 1 of this act, which petition shall set forth and particularly describe the proposed boundaries of such district and shall pray that the same may be organized under the provisions of this act. The petitioners must accompany the petition with a good and sufficient bond to be approved by the said board of county commissioners. in double the amount of the probable cost of organizing such district, conditioned that the bondsmen will pay all said costs in case said organization shall not be effected. Such petition shall be filed in the office of the county clerk and a notice thereof shall be published for at least two weeks before the time at which the same is to be presented to the board of county commissioners in some newspaper printed and published in the county where said petition is presented, which newspaper shall be designated by said board as the paper most likely to impart notice of the hearing of said petition; the said notice to set forth that said petition has been filed, the time of the meeting of said board to consider said petition, and a description of the territory to be embraced in such proposed district.

SEC. 3. When such petition is presented, and it shall appear that the notice of the presentation of said petition has been given and that said petition has been signed by the requisite number of petitioners as required by this act, the commissioners shall hold a hearing on said petition and may adjourn such hearing from time to time not exceeding three weeks in all. Contiguous or neighboring lands susceptible of irrigation from the common source or combined sources aforesaid, not included in such district as described in the petition, may at such hearing upon application of the holder or holders of title or evidence of title thereto as prescribed in section 1 hereof be included in such district, and lands described in said petition not susceptible of irrigation from such system or systems may upon similar application be excluded therefrom; *provided always,* that said board shall not modify the boundaries described in the petition so as to change the object of said petition or so as to exempt from the operation of this act any land which is susceptible of irrigation by the system or systems aforesaid. In the hearing of any such petition the board of county commissioners shall disregard any informalities therein, and in case it deny the same or dismiss it for any reasons on account of the provisions of this act not having been complied with, which are the only reasons upon which it shall have the right to refuse or dismiss the same, it shall state its reasons in writing therefor in detail, which shall be entered upon its records, and in case the reasons are not well founded a writ of mandamus shall upon proper application therefor issue out of the district court of the county compelling it to act in compliance with this act, which writ shall be heard within twenty days from the date of issuance, such time to be excluded from the time given the county commissioners to act upon the petition. Upon the completion of the hearing the county commissioners shall forthwith make an order denying or granting the prayer of said petition, and if the same is granted shall, in said order, define and establish the boundaries and designate the name of such proposed district and divide the same into three, five, or seven divisions, as prescribed in the petition, as nearly equal in size as may be practicable. Thereupon the said commissioners shall by further order duly entered upon their record call an election of the qualified electors of said proposed district to determine whether such district shall be organized under the provisions of this act, and by such order shall submit the names of one or more persons from each of the divisions of said district to be voted for as directors of the district. One director shall be elected from each division and shall be a qualified elector of the district and holder of title, or evidence of title, as prescribed in section 1 of this act, to land within the division from which he is elected. Each division shall constitute an election precinct for the purposes of this act. The board of county commissioners shall give notice of such election, which shall be published for two weeks prior to such election in a newspaper within the county where the petition is filed. Such notice shall require the electors to cast ballots, which shall contain the words "Irrigation District—Yes," or "Irrigation District—No," or words equivalent thereto, and the names of persons to be voted for as directors. For the purpose of this election the board shall establish a polling place in each election precinct aforesaid, and shall also appoint three qualified electors to act as inspectors of election in each election precinct, and also appoint for each precinct two clerks of election. The number of directors and the number and boundaries of divisions of any district organized under the laws of this state shall not be altered or changed except by a petition of a majority of the qualified electors of the district and a majority of the directors.

SEC. 4. Except as in this act otherwise provided, all such elections shall be conducted as near as may be practicable in accordance with the general election laws of this state. The board of county commissioners shall meet on the second Monday succeeding such election and proceed to canvass the votes cast thereat, and if upon such canvass it appear that a majority of the electors voted "Irrigation District—Yes" the board, by an order entered upon its minutes, shall declare such territory duly organized as an irrigation district under the name and style theretofore designated, and shall declare the persons receiving respectively the highest number of votes for directors to be duly elected, and shall cause a copy of such order and a plat of said district, each duly certified by the clerk of the board of county commissioners, to be immediately filed for record in the office of the county recorder of each county in which any portion of such lands are situated, and certified copies thereof shall also be filed with the county clerk of such counties, and thereafter the organization of the district shall be complete. No lands while they remain within a district shall be included in any other district.

SEC. 5. The regular elections of irrigation districts shall be held on the first Tuesday after the first Monday in April of the second calendar year after the completion of the organization thereof, and on the same day biennially thereafter, or as to districts heretofore organized, biennially after the first regular election therein. The directors elected at the organization election shall be selected by lot so that one, two or three directors, according to whether there are in all three, five, or seven on the board, shall hold office until their successors are elected at the next regular election and qualify, and two, three, or four directors, as the case may be, shall hold office until their successors are elected at the second regular election after organization and qualify, and at the regular election biennially thereafter directors shall be elected, to replace the directors whose terms expire, for terms of four years, or until their successors are elected and qualify. Directors so elected shall have the qualifications prescribed in this act for directors elected at the time of organization. Nominations for the office of directors shall be made by filing a declaration with the secretary within fifty days before the date of election and not later than ten days before such election. Candidates shall pay twenty-five ($25) dollars filing fee with such declaration.

SEC. 6. Not less than fifteen nor more than twenty days before any election held under this act subsequent to the organization of the district the secretary shall cause notice specifying the polling places and time of holding the election to be posted in three public places in each election precinct and in the office of the board of directors. Prior to the time for posting the notice the board of directors shall appoint three qualified electors to act as inspectors of election in such election precinct and shall also appoint two clerks of election for each precinct. If the board of directors fail to appoint a board of election or the members appointed do not attend the opening of the polls on the morning of election the electors of the precinct present at that hour may appoint the board or supply the place of absent members thereof. The board of directors shall, in its order appointing the board of election, designate the hour and the place in each precinct where the election shall be held. At least four weeks before any such election said board of directors shall appoint a registrar for each precinct of the district. Such registrars shall be governed in the performance of their duties by the general election laws of the state as far as they are applicable and shall be at their places of registration to receive applications for registrations from nine o'clock a. m. to nine o'clock p. m. on each of the three Saturdays next preceding the date of election. The registrars shall require registrants to take the following oath, in substance: "I am, or have declared my intention to become, a citizen of the United States, am over the age of twenty-one years, and am, or properly represent, under the law in pursuance of which this election is to be held, the holder of title or evidence of title, as defined in said law, to land within the boundaries of the .... irrigation district." No election for any purpose except for organization shall be held in any irrigation district without such registration, and only electors duly registered shall be entitled to vote thereat.

SEC. 7. Before opening the polls each inspector and each clerk must take and subscribe to an oath to faithfully perform the duties imposed upon him by law. Any elector of the precinct may administer and certify such oath. Vacancies occurring during the progress of the election may be filled by the remaining inspector or inspectors, and any inspector of election may administer and certify oaths. The time of opening and closing the polls, the manner of conducting the election, canvassing and announcing the result, the keeping of the tally-list, and the making and certifying of such result and the disposition of the ballots after election shall be the same, as near as may be, as provided for elections under the general election law of this state, but no registrar or election officer shall receive any pay for services at any district election. The returns shall be delivered to the secretary of the district and no list, tally-paper or returns from any election shall be set aside or rejected for want of form if it can be satisfactorily understood. The board of directors shall meet at its usual place of meeting on the second Monday after an election to canvass the returns and it shall proceed in the same manner and with like effect, as near as may be, as the board of county commissioners in canvassing the returns of general elections, and when it shall have declared the result the secretary shall make full entries in his record in like manner as is required of the county clerk in general elections. The board of directors must declare elected the person or persons having the highest number of votes given for each office. The secretary shall immediately make out and deliver to such person or persons a certificate of election signed by him and authenticated with the seal of the board. Within ten days after receiving the certificate of his election, each director shall take and subscribe to an official oath and file the same with the secretary of the board of directors. Each member of said board of directors shall execute an official bond in the sum of fifteen thousand dollars ($15,000), which shall be approved by the judge of the district court in and for the county where such organization is effected. Such bonds shall be recorded in the office of the county recorder and filed with the secretary of the board.

SEC. 8. Any person, male or female, of the age of 21 years or over, whether a resident of the district or not, who is or has declared his intention to become a citizen of the United States and who is a bona-fide holder of title, or evidence of title, as defined in section 1 hereof, to land situated in the district, shall be entitled to one vote at any election held under the provisions of this act, and shall be held to be referred to whenever the words elector or electors are used herein. Any elector residing outside of the district owning land in the district and qualified to vote at district elections shall be considered as a resident of that division and precinct on of his lands are located for the purpose of determining his place of voting and qualifications for holding office. A guardian, executor or administrator shall be considered as the holder of title or evidence of title as prescribed in section 1 hereof to the land in the estate for which he is such guardian, executor, or administrator, and shall have the right to sign petitions, vote and do all things that any elector may or can do under this act. Corporations holding land in the district shall be considered as persons entitled to exercise all the rights of natural persons and the president of the corporation, or other person duly authorized by the president or vice-president in writing, may sign any petition authorized by this act or cast the vote of the corporation at any election.

Sec. 9. The officers of such district shall consist of three, five, or seven directors, as aforesaid, a president and vice-president elected from their number, a secretary and a treasurer. The secretary and treasurer shall be appointed by the board of directors and may or may not be members of said board. Such officers shall serve at the will of the board. One person may be appointed to serve as secretary and treasurer. The board of directors shall designate some place within the county where the organization of the district was effected as the office of the board and the board shall hold a regular monthly meeting in its office on the first Monday in every month and such special meetings as may be required for the proper transaction of business; *provided*, that all special meetings must be called by the president or a majority of the board. The order calling such special meeting shall be entered of record, and the secretary shall give each member not joining in the order five days' notice of such special meeting. The order must specify the business to be transacted at such special meeting, and none other than that specified shall be transacted. Whenever all members of the board are present at a meeting the same shall be deemed a legal meeting and any lawful business may be transacted. All meetings of the board shall be public and a majority of the members shall constitute a quorum for the transaction of business, but on all questions requiring a vote there shall be a concurrence of at least a majority of the members of the board. All records of the board shall be open to the inspection of any elector during business hours. On the first Monday in May next following their election, the board of directors shall meet and organize, elect a president and vice-president and appoint a secretary and treasurer. The appointees aforesaid shall file bonds which shall be approved by the board, for the faithful performance of their duties. Any vacancies in the office of director shall be filled from the division in which the vacancy occurs by the remaining members of the board. A director appointed to fill a vacancy, as above provided, shall hold his office for the unexpired term of his predecessor in office, and until his successor is elected and qualifies.

SEC. 10. The board of directors shall have power to manage and conduct the business and affairs of the district, to make and execute all necessary contracts, to employ and appoint such agents, officers, and employees as may be required and prescribe their duties, and to establish by-laws, rules and regulations for the distribution and use of water in the district. Said by-laws, rules, and regulations shall be printed in convenient form for distribution throughout the district. For the purpose of acquiring control over government lands within the district, and of complying with the provisions of the aforesaid act of Congress of August 11, 1916, the board shall have power to make such investigation and base thereon such representations and assurances to the secretary of the interior as may be requisite. The board and its agents and employees shall have the right to enter upon any land to make surveys, and may locate the necessary irrigation and other works, and the lines of any canal or canals, and the necessary branches for the same, on any lands which may be deemed best for such location. Said board shall also have the right to acquire, either by purchase, condemnation, or other legal means, all lands, rights, and other property necessary for the construction, use and supply, operation, maintenance, repair, and improvement of the works of the district, including canals and works constructed and being constructed by private owners, lands for reservoirs for the storage of waters, and all other works and appurtenances, either within or without the State of Nevada. In case of purchase of property the bonds of the district hereinafter provided for may be used to their par value in payment. The board may appropriate water in accordance with the law, and also construct the necessary dams, reservoirs, and works for the collection, storage, conservation and distribution of water for said district and for the drainage of the lands thereof; and do any and every lawful act necessary to be done in order to accomplish the things and purposes herein described. The collection, storage, conveyance, distribution and use of water by or through the works of irrigation districts heretofore or hereafter organized, together with the rights of way for canals and ditches, sites for reservoirs, and all other works and property required to fully carry out the provisions of this act, is hereby declared to be a public use.

SEC. 11. The said board is hereby authorized and empowered to institute, maintain, and defend, in the name of the district, any and all actions and proceedings, suits at law, and in equity.

SEC. 12. The members of the board of directors shall each receive five dollars per day and actual traveling expenses for each day spent attending meetings of said board or while engaged in official business under the order of the board. The board shall fix the compensation to be paid to the other officers named in this act; *provided,* that said board shall, upon the petition of a majority of the electors within such district, submit to the electors at any general election of said district a schedule of salaries and fees to be paid the direc- tors and officers thereof. Such petitions shall be presented to the board twenty days prior to such general election and a schedule fee submitted upon a two-thirds vote therefor shall be put into effect upon the first of the month next ensuing.

SEC. 13. No director or any other officer named in this act shall in any manner be interested, directly or indirectly, in any contract awarded by the board, or in the profits to be derived therefrom; and for any violation of this provi- sion such officer shall be deemed guilty of a misdemeanor, and upon conviction thereof shall suffer a forfeiture of his office, and he shall be punished by a fine not exceeding five hundred dollars, or by imprisonment in the county jail not to exceed six months or by both such fine and imprisonment.

SEC. 14. The board of directors, or other officers of the district, shall have no power to incur any debt or liability whatever either by issuing bonds or otherwise in excess of the express provisions of this act, and any debt or liability incurred in excess of such express provisions shall be and remain absolutely void; *provided,* that for the purpose of organization, or for any of the purposes of this act, the board of directors may, before the collection of the first assessment, incur an indebtedness not exceeding in the aggregate the sum of three thousand dollars, and may cause warrants of the district to issue therefor, bearing interest at six per cent per annum, and the directors shall have the right and power to levy an assessment of not to exceed ten (10) cents per acre on all lands in said district for the payment of such expenses. Thereafter the directors shall have the right and power to levy an assessment, annually, in the absence of assessments therefor under any of the other provisions of this act of not to exceed ten (10) cents per acre on all lands in said district for the payment of the ordinary and current expenses of the district, including salaries of officers and other incidental expenses. Such assessments shall be collected as in this act provided for the collection of other assessments.

SEC. 15. As soon as practicable after the organization of a district the board of directors shall, by a resolution entered on its records, formulate a general plan of its proposed operations in which it shall state what constructed works or other property it proposes to purchase and the cost of pur- chasing the same, and also what construction work it pro- poses to do, and how it proposes to raise the funds for

carrying out such general plan. The board shall cause such surveys and examinations to be made as will furnish a proper basis for an estimate of the cost of carrying out the construction work. All such surveys, examinations, maps, plans, and estimates shall be made under the direction of a competent irrigation engineer and certified by him. Upon receiving his report the board shall proceed to determine the amount of money necessary to be raised for the purchase of property and construction of works; and shall immediately thereafter call a special election at which shall be submitted to the electors of said district possessing the qualifications prescribed by this act the question whether or not the expense shall be authorized and whether by bond issue or otherwise. Notice of such election must be given by posting notices in three public places in each election precinct in the district for three weeks before the date of election, and the publication thereof for three weeks in some newspaper published in the county where the district was organized. Such notice shall specify the time of holding the election, the amount of bonds proposed to be issued, and shall state in substance that such plans and estimates as have been made are on file for inspection by the electors of the district at the office of the board. Said election must be held and the result thereof determined and declared in all respects as nearly as practicable in conformity with the provisions of this act governing the election of officers, and no informalities in conducting such an election shall invalidate the same if it shall have been otherwise fairly conducted. At such an election the ballot shall contain the words "..........................
(Question) Yes," or "................................... (Question) No," or words equivalent thereto. If two-thirds or more of the votes cast are "Yes," the board of directors shall be authorized to incur the expense, and if a bond issue be authorized shall cause bonds in the amount authorized to be issued. If more than one-third of the votes cast at any bond election are "No," the result of such election shall be so declared and entered of record. Thereafter, whenever said board in its judgment deems it for the best interest of the district that the question of the issuance of bonds in such amount, or in any other amount, shall be submitted to the electors it shall so declare of record in its minutes, and may thereupon submit such question to said electors in the same manner and with like effect as at such previous election, but no question shall be resubmitted to the electors within one year after the same has been voted upon and rejected.

SEC. 16. The bonds authorized by vote shall be designated as a series, and the series shall be numbered consecutively as authorized. The portion of the bonds of the series sold at any time shall be designated as an issue and each issue shall be numbered in its order. The bonds of such issue shall be numbered consecutively, commencing with those earliest falling due, and they shall be designated as eleven-year bonds, twelve-year bonds, etc. They shall be negotiable in form, and payable in money of the United States as follows, to wit: At the expiration of eleven years from each issue, five per cent of the whole number of bonds of such issue; at the expiration of twelve years, six per cent; at the expiration of thirteen years, seven per cent; at the expiration of fourteen years, eight per cent; at the expiration of fifteen years, nine per cent; at the expiration of sixteen years, ten per cent; at the expiration of seventeen years, eleven per cent; at the expiration of eighteen years, thirteen per cent; at the expiration of nineteen years, fifteen per cent; at the expiration of twenty years, sixteen per cent; *provided,* that such percentage may be changed sufficiently so that every bond shall be in the amount of one hundred dollars, or a multiple thereof, and the above provisions shall not be construed to require any single bond to fall due in partial payments. Interest coupons shall be attached thereto, and all bonds and coupons shall be dated on January 1, or July 1, next following the date of their authorization, and they shall bear interest at the rate of not to exceed six per cent per annum, payable semiannually on the first day of January and July of each year. The principal and interest shall be payable at the place designated therein. Said bonds shall be each of a denomination of not less than one hundred dollars, nor more than one thousand dollars, and shall be signed by the president and secretary, and the seal of the district shall be affixed thereto. Coupons attached to each bond shall be signed by the secretary. Said bonds shall express on their face that they were issued by the authority of this act, naming it, and shall also state the number of the issue of which said bonds are a part. The secretary and the treasurer shall each keep a record of the bonds sold, their number, the date of sale, the price received, and the name of the purchaser. In case the money raised by the sale of all the bonds be insufficient for the completion of the plans and works adopted, and additional bonds be not voted, it shall be the duty of the board of directors to provide for the completion of said plan by levy or assessment therefor; *provided, further,* that when the money obtained by any previous issue of bonds has become exhausted by expenditures herein authorized, and it becomes necessary to raise additional moneys to carry out the adopted plan, additional bonds may be issued if authorized at an election for that purpose, which election shall be called and otherwise conducted in accordance with the provisions of this act in respect to an original issue of bonds. The lien for taxes for the payment of interest and principal of any bond issue shall be a prior lien to that of any subsequent bond issue. The time for the issuance and maturity of the bonds and the manner of their payment may be otherwise determined and directed, if submitted to a vote, by the electors of said district at the election authorizing the said bonds.

SEC. 17. Whenever the electors shall have authorized an issue of bonds, as hereinbefore provided, the board of directors shall examine each tract or legal subdivision of land in the district, and shall determine the benefits which will accrue to each of such tracts or subdivisions from the construction or purchase of the works proposed for the district; and the costs of such works shall be apportioned or distributed over such tracts or subdivisions of land in proportion to such benefits. The board shall make, or cause to be made, a list of such apportionment or distribution, which list shall contain a complete description of each subdivision or tract of land of such district with the amount and rate per acre of such apportionment or distribution, and the name of the owner thereof, or it may prepare a map on a convenient scale showing each of said subdivisions or tracts with the rate per acre of such apportionment entered thereon; *provided,* that where all or any portion of the lands are assessed by said board at the same rate a general statement to that effect shall be sufficient. Said list or map shall be made in duplicate, and one copy of each shall be filed in the office of the state engineer, and the original shall remain in the office of the board of directors. Whenever thereafter an assessment is made, either in lieu of bonds, or an annual assessment for raising the interest on bonds, or any portion of the principal, or the expenses of maintaining the property of the district, or any special assessment voted by the electors, it shall be spread upon the lands in the same proportion as the assessments of benefits, and the whole amount of the assessments of benefits shall equal the amount of bonds or other obligations authorized at the election last above mentioned; *provided always,* that the benefits arising from the undertakings for which special assessments are made may be distributed equally over the lands, or especially apportioned, when such course is authorized in the election therefor, and that assessments or tolls and charges may be made or imposed as hereinafter provided, when coming within the designation of operation and maintenance charges, by way of a minimum stated charge per acre whether water is used or not, and a charge for water used in excess of the amount delivered for the minimum charge, or such other reasonable method of fixing or collecting the operation and maintenance charge as the board of directors may adopt. Where drainage works are to be constructed, benefits may be apportioned to higher lands not then actually requiring drainage by reason of the fact that their irrigation contributes water which must be carried off or away from the lower lands.

SEC. 18. Before final action upon the apportionment of benefits provided for in the last preceding section, the board shall publish notice for two weeks in a newspaper published in the county in which the organization was effected that it will meet at its office on the day stated in said notice for the purpose of reviewing such apportionment of benefits. At such meeting the board shall proceed to hear all parties interested who may appear, and it shall continue in session from day to day until the apportionment is completed. It shall hear and receive all evidence offered, including any maps or surveys which any owners of lands may produce, and may classify the lands in such a way that the assessment when completed shall be just and equitable. Any person interested who shall fail to appear before the board shall not be permitted thereafter to contest said apportionment, or any assessment thereunder, except upon a special application to the court in the proceeding for confirmation of said apportionment, showing reasonable excuse for failing to appear before the board. In case any elector makes objection to said apportionment before said board, and said objection is overruled and such elector does not consent to the apportionment as finally determined, such objection shall, without further proceedings, be heard at the confirmation proceedings herein provided for.

Sec. 19. The board of directors of the district shall file with the clerk of the district court in and for the county in which its office is situated, a petition praying in effect that the proceedings aforesaid be examined, approved and confirmed by the court. The petition shall state generally that the irrigation district was duly organized and the first board of directors elected, that due and legal proceedings were taken to issue bonds, stating the amount thereof, and that an apportionment of benefits was made by the board and a list thereof duly filed according to law. A list of the apportionment shall be attached to said petition, but the petition need not state other facts. Such petition for confirmation of the proceedings thus far had may be filed after the organization of the district is complete, or after the authorization of any issue of bonds, or after any other undertaking of the district. The court or judge shall fix the time and place for the hearing of any such petition, and the clerk shall publish a notice thereof for two consecutive weeks in a newspaper published in the county. Any person interested may on or before the day fixed for said hearing answer said petition. None of the pleadings need be sworn to, and every material statement of the petition not controverted by answer shall be taken as true. A failure to answer the petition shall be deemed to be an admission of the material allegations thereof. The rules of pleading and practice provided by the civil practice act of this state shall be followed so far as applicable. A motion for a new trial, and all proceedings in the nature of appeals or rehearings, may be had as in any ordinary civil action.

Sec. 20. Upon the hearing of such petition, the court shall examine all the proceedings sought to be confirmed and may ratify, approve and confirm the same or any part thereof; and when an apportionment of benefits is examined all objections thereto, including those made at the hearing before the board, shall be set up in the answer and heard by the court. The court shall disregard every error, irregularity or omission which does not affect the substantial rights of any party, and if the court shall find that the apportionment is as to any substantial matter erroneous or unjust, the same shall not be returned to the board, but the court shall proceed to correct the same so as to conform to this act and the rights of all parties in the premises, and the final judgment may approve and confirm such proceedings in whole or in part. In case of the approval of the organization of the district and the disapproval of the proceedings for issuing bonds the district may again undertake proceedings for the issuance of bonds and have the same confirmed as herein provided. The cost of the proceedings in court may be allowed and apportioned among the parties thereto in the discretion of the court.

SEC. 21. The board may sell bonds from time to time in such quantities as may be necessary and most advantageous to raise money for the construction of works and the acquisition of property and rights and to otherwise carry out the objects and purposes of this act. Before making any sale the board shall by resolution declare its intention to sell a specific number and amount of bonds, and if said bonds can be sold at par with accrued interest they may be disposed of without advertising; otherwise notice shall be published for three weeks in a newspaper in the county in which the office of the district is situated, and in such other newspaper in or outside of the state as the board may deem expedient. that sealed proposals will be received at its office on or before a day and hour set in said notice for the purchase of said bonds. At the time appointed the board shall publicly open the proposals, and sell the bonds to the highest responsible bidder, or it may reject all bids; but in case no bids are received, or all bids are rejected, it shall not again be necessary to advertise the sale thereof, but they may be sold at any time until canceled; *provided,* that the said board shall in no event sell any of the bonds for less than ninety (90) per cent of the par value thereof and accrued interest. If for any reason the bonds of a district cannot be sold, or if at any time it shall be deemed for the best interests of the district to withdraw from sale all or any portion of an authorized bond issue, the board of directors may, in its discretion, cancel the same and levy assessments in the amount of the bonds canceled; *provided,* that the revenue derived from said assessments must be employed for the same purpose as was contemplated by the bond authorization, but no levy shall be made to pay for work or material, payment for which was contemplated by bonds which have been authorized, until bonds to the amount of said assessments have been canceled. Assessments made in lieu of bonds canceled shall be collected in the same manner and shall have the same force and effect as other assesments levied under the provisions of this act; *provided,* that such assessments shall not during any one year exceed ten per cent of the total bond issue authorized by such district, unless a greater assessment shall be authorized by a majority vote of the qualified electors of the district voting at a general election or a special election called for that purpose.

SEC. 22. Said bonds and the interest thereon shall be paid by revenue derived from the annual assessment upon the lands in the district; and all the land in the district shall be and remain liable to be assessed for such payment in accord with the apportionment of benefits as in this act provided.

SEC. 23. The following funds are hereby created and established, to which the moneys properly belonging shall be apportioned, to wit: Construction fund, bond fund, and general fund. Moneys accruing from the sale of bonds, and from any assessments levied for the direct payment of cost of construction, purchase of property, or other undertakings for which bonds may be issued, shall be deposited and kept in the construction fund. Moneys accruing from assessments levied for the payment of interest and principal on bonds shall be deposited and kept in the bond fund. All other moneys, including those realized from assessments, or, as the case may be, from tolls and charges levied or imposed for defraying the organization and current expense of the district, and expenses and cost of the care, operation, maintenance, management, repair, and necessary current improvement or replacement of existing works and property, including salaries and wages of officers and employees and other proper incidental expenditures, shall be deposited and kept in the general fund. The treasurer of the district is hereby authorized and required to receive and receipt for and to collect the moneys accruing to the several funds above named, and to place the same to the credit of the district in the appropriate fund. Said treasurer shall be responsible upon his official bond for the safe-keeping and disbursement of the moneys in such funds. Interest coupons shall be paid by him as in this act provided. The board may establish rules and regulations and prescribe the conditions under which the treasurer may make disbursements from the general fund, but no other payments from any of the funds above named shall be made by the treasurer except upon vouchers signed by the president and secretary authorized by order of the board. The county treasurer or treasurers who are required by this act to collect assessments levied by the district are hereby authorized to turn over to the treasurer of the district all moneys so collected and to take his receipt therefor. Such district treasurer shall report to the board in writing on the first Monday in each month the amount of money in the several funds aforesaid and the amounts received and paid out in the preceding month, and the treasurer shall make such other report and accounting as the board may require. Such reports shall be verified and filed with the secretary of the board.

SEC. 24. The treasurer, upon the presentation of interest coupons when due, shall pay the same from the bond fund. Whenever after ten years from the issuance of bonds said fund shall amount to the sum of ten thousand dollars, the board of directors may direct the treasurer to pay such an amount of said bonds not due as the money in said fund will redeem at the lowest value at which they may be offered for liquidation, after advertising for at least three weeks in some newspaper published in the county in which the office of the district is located, and in such other newspapers as the board may deem advisable, for sealed proposals for the redemption of such bonds. Such proposals shall be opened by the board in open meeting at a time to be named in the notice, and the lowest bid or bids shall be accepted; *provided,* that no bonds shall be redeemed at a rate above par. In case two or more bids are equal the lowest-numbered bond shall have the preference, and if any of said bonds are not so redeemed, that amount of the redemption money shall be invested by the treasurer under the direction of the board in United States bonds or the bonds or warrants of the state or municipal or school bonds, and such bonds and the proceeds therefrom shall belong to the bond fund.

SEC. 25. The secretary of the board of directors shall be the assessor of the district and on or before August fifteenth of each year shall prepare an assessment book containing a full and accurate list and description of all the land of the district, and a list of the persons who own, claim or have possession or control thereof during said year, giving the number of acres listed to each person. If the name of the person owning, claiming, possessing, or controlling any tract of said land is not known, it shall be listed to "unknown owner."

SEC. 26. The board shall meet on the first Monday in September of each year to correct assessments and the secretary shall publish notice of such meeting for two weeks in a newspaper published in the county in which the district was organized. In the meantime the assessment book or books shall remain in the office of the secretary for the inspection of all parties interested. The board of directors, which is hereby constituted a board of correction for the purpose. shall meet and continue from day to day as long as may be necessary, not to exceed five days, exclusive of holidays, and may make such changes in said assessment book or books as may be necessary to have it conform to the facts. Within ten days after the close of said session the secretary of the board shall have the corrected assessment book or books completed.

SEC. 27. At its regular meeting in October the board of directors shall levy an assessment upon the lands in said district in accordance with the provisions of this act, which assessment shall be sufficient to raise the annual interest on the outstanding bonds. At the expiration of ten years after a bond issue or such other period as may be authorized, the board must increase said assessment as may be necessary from year to year to raise a sum sufficient to pay the principal of the outstanding bonds of that issue as they mature. The secretary of the board shall compute and enter in a separate column of the assessment book or books the respective sums to be paid as an assessment on the property therein enumerated. Except as otherwise provided herein, assessments made for any of the other purposes of this act shall be made and levied as above provided and entered in appropriate columns of the assessment book or books.

SEC. 28. An assessment is a lien against the property assessed from and after the first Monday in March of the succeeding year. The lien of the bonds of any issue shall be a preferred lien to that of any subsequent issue, and such lien is not removed until the assessments are paid or the property sold for the payment thereof. •

SEC. 29. An assessment book shall be made up for the lands in each county in which the district is situated and the secretary of the board of directors shall forthwith certify the same to the county auditor or county auditors, as the case may be, who shall enter such assessments in the tax rolls of such county or counties. The assessments when levied and enrolled shall become due and delinquent at the same time and be subject to the same penalties and shall be collected by the same officers and in the same manner as state and county taxes. The county auditor, district attorney, clerk and treasurer shall do and perform all acts necessary to accomplish the collection of the same with penalties and the sale for delinquency and redemption of the lands involved.

SEC. 30. After adopting a plan for such works as are proposed, and then there is sufficient money in the construction fund as aforesaid, the board of directors shall cause notice to be given by the secretary by publication thereof for not less than two weeks in a newspaper published in the county in which the district was organized, and in such other publications or newspapers as it may deem advisable, calling for bids for the construction of such works, or any portion thereof. If less than the whole work is advertised then the portions so advertised must be particularly described in such notice. The notice shall set forth that the plans and specifications can be seen at the office of the board, that the board will receive sealed proposals for the construction of the proposed works and that a contract therefor will be let to the lowest responsible bidder, subject to the right of the board to reject any and all bids, stating the time and place for opening the bids. At the time and place appointed the bids shall be opened in public and as soon as convenient thereafter the board shall accept a bid or bids and contract for the construction of the works, either in portions or as a whole, or it may reject any and all bids and readvertise for proposals. Contracts for the purchase of material shall be entered into in the same manner, but if no reasonable bid is received the material may be purchased without advertisement. Any person or persons to whom a contract may be awarded shall enter into a bond in favor of the district with good and sufficient sureties, to be approved by the board for not less than 20 per cent of the amount of the contract price, conditioned upon the faithful performance of said contract. The work shall be done under the direction and to the satisfaction of the engineer employed by the district and approved by the board; *provided,* that no contract of any kind shall be let by said board of directors unless there is sufficient money in the district treasury at the time such contract is let to fully pay for the work or material so contracted for.

SEC. 31. On the petition of a majority of the electors of the district, the board of directors may do any work mentioned in the preceding section on behalf of the district without calling for bids, and it may use the construction fund therefor.

SEC. 32. The cost and expense of purchasing and acquiring property, and of constructing works to carry out the formulated plan or plans, whether for irrigation or drainage or both, or for the improvement or supplementing of existing works, except as otherwise provided herein, shall be paid out of the construction fund. For the purpose of defraying the organization and current expense of the district, and of the care, operation, maintenance, management, repair, and necessary current improvement or replacement of existing works and property, including salaries and wages of officers and employees and other proper incidental expenditures, the board may fix rates of tolls or charges, and provide for the collection thereof by the district treasurer as operation and maintenance, or some like designation, or may levy assessments therefor, or for a portion thereof, collecting the balance as tolls or charges as aforesaid. In this relation provision may be made by the board for the fixing, levying and collection of a minimum, flat, or stated operation and maintenance assessment, toll, or charge per acre, whether water is used or not, and a further operation and maintenance toll or charge for water used in excess of the amount delivered for the minimum charge; or the board may adopt other reasonable methods of fixing and collecting the operation and maintenance charges. Assessments, tolls, and charges may be collected in advance, and the assessment aforesaid, and such tolls and charges, may be based upon an estimate of the operation and maintenance revenue required for the current or ensuing year; to be adjusted as near as may be from year to year. Water service may be refused and water delivery may be shut off whenever there is a default in the payment of operation and maintenance, but all other legal remedies shall also be available for the enforcement of the debt. The tolls and charges shall be collected by the treasurer and deposited in the general fund, and he shall account therefor and disburse the same as in this act provided.

SEC. 33. The board of directors shall have the power to construct the works of the district across any stream of water, watercourse, street, avenue, highway, railway, canal, ditch or flume, in such manner as to afford security for life and property; but said board shall restore the same when so crossed or intersected to their former state as near as may be or in a manner not unnecessarily impairing its usefulness; and if a railroad company or those in control of the property, thing or franchise to be crossed cannot agree with the board upon the amount to be paid, or upon the point or points or the manner of crossing or intersecting, the same shall be ascertained and determined as herein provided in respect to the taking of land.

SEC. 34. The right of way is hereby given, dedicated and set apart, to locate, construct, operate, and maintain the works of the district over and through any of the lands which are now or may be the property of the state.

SEC. 35. All irrigation districts organized under the laws of the State of Nevada shall have the right of eminent domain with the power by and through their board of directors to cause to be condemned and appropriated in the name of and for the use of said districts all reservoirs, canals, and works, with their appurtenances, constructed for the irrigation or drainage of any lands within the district for uses incidental thereto, and all lands required therefor, and all lands and rights of way required for the works constructed, or to be constructed, or which may be acquired by the district, and all necessary appurtenances and other property and rights necessary for the construction, operation, maintenance, repair, and improvement of said works. Such districts shall have the right by and through their boards of directors to acquire by purchase or other legal means any or all of the property mentioned and referred to in this section. In any action or proceedings for the condemnation of any such property wherein an irrigation district is plaintiff such district, within six months after final judgment, shall pay the amount awarded in the judgment or said judgment will be annulled. Except as otherwise provided in this act, the provisions of the laws of Nevada relative to the right of eminent domain, civil actions, new trials and appeals, shall be applicable to and constitute the rules of practice in condemnation proceedings by irrigation districts.

SEC. 36. The holder or holders of any title or evidence of title, as defined in section 1 hereof, representing one-half or more of any body of lands adjacent to or in the vicinity of an irrigation district, which are susceptible of irrigation or drainage, as the case may be, or both, by the district system, or combined systems of works, may file with the board of directors of the district a petition, in writing, praying that said land may be annexed. The petition shall describe the land and also describe the several parcels owned by petitioners.

SEC. 37. The secretary shall cause a notice of the filing of such petition to be published two weeks in a newspaper published in the county where the district was organized. The notice shall state the filing of such petition, the names of the petitioners, and contain a description of the lands mentioned in the petition, sufficient to identify the same, and it shall notify all persons interested in or that may be affected by such change of boundaries of the district to appear at the office of the board at a time named in said notice and show cause in writing, if any they have, why the lands mentioned should not be annexed to said district. The petitioner or petitioners shall advance to the district treasurer sufficient money to pay the estimated cost of these proceedings.

SEC. 38. The board of directors, at the time mentioned in said notice, or at such other time to which the hearing may be adjourned, shall hear the petition and all the objections thereto. The failure of any person to show cause as aforesaid shall be taken as an assent on his part to a change of the boundaries of the district so as to include the whole or part of the land mentioned in the petition.

SEC. 39. The board of directors may require as a condition to the granting of said petition that the petitioners shall pay to the district such sums as nearly as the same can be estimated as said petitioners or their grantors would theretofore have been required to pay had such lands been included in such district at the time the same was originally organized.

SEC. 40. The board of directors, if they deem it not for the best interests of the district to include therein the lands mentioned in the petition shall reject the same. But if the board deem it for the best interests of the district, and if no person interested shall show cause why the proposed change be not made, or if having shown cause withdraws the same, the board may order, without any election, that the lands mentioned in said petition or any part thereof be annexed to the district. The order shall describe the lands so annexed, and the board shall cause a survey thereof to be made if deemed necessary.

SEC. 41. If any person interested shall object as aforesaid and shall not withdraw the same, and if the board deem it for the best interests of the district to include the lands mentioned in said objection, or some part thereof, the board shall adopt a resolution to that effect. The resolution shall describe the lands proposed to be included in the district.

SEC. 42. Upon the adoption of the resolution mentioned in the last preceding section the board shall order that an election be held within said district to determine whether the lands described in said resolution shall be annexed to the district, and shall fix the time at which such election shall be held. Notice thereof shall be published, and such election shall be held, and all things pertaining thereto conducted in the manner prescribed by this act in case of an election to determine whether bonds of the district shall be issued. The ballots cast at such election shall contain the words "for annexation," or "against annexation," or expressions equivalent thereto. The notice of election shall describe the lands proposed to be annexed to the district.

SEC. 43. If at such election a majority of all the votes cast shall be against annexation the board shall proceed no further in the matter; but if a majority of such votes be in favor of annexation the board shall thereupon order that the boundaries of the district be changed to include the lands to be so annexed and cause a copy of such order, together with a plat of said lands, each certified to by the secretary of the board, to be filed for record in the office of the county recorder of the county or counties in which such lands are situated. The order shall describe the land so annexed and thereafter such lands shall be subject to all the provisions of this act. Immediately after the filing for record of the order annexing said lands the directors shall state on their minutes to which division or divisions in said district the lands shall be attached, or may redivide the district to accommodate said lands.

SEC. 44. The holder or holders of title, or evidence of title, as described in section 1 hereof, may file with the board of directors a petition, in writing, praying that the boundaries of said district be so changed as to exclude the lands described therein. The petition shall describe the boundaries of the several parcels owned by the petitioners and shall state the reasons for the exclusion prayed for. The board of directors shall cause the land described in such petition to be surveyed and reported upon by a competent irrigation engineer, and if the board shall then find said lands to be of such character as to prevent their receiving benefits from the existing or proposed works, the board shall make an order changing the boundaries of said district so as to exclude the land described in said petition. If lands are excluded as in this section provided a copy of the order excluding same, with a plat of land excluded, each certified by the secretary of the board, shall be filed for record in the office of the county recorder of the county or counties in which such lands are situated. If said petition be denied, the signers thereof shall be liable to the district for the full amount of cost of the proceedings and survey of said lands.

SEC. 45. No state lands shall become a part of an irrigation district except by the consent of the state land register, who is hereby authorized to consent thereto on behalf of the state in writing when in his judgment, with the advice of the state engineer, such lands will be benefited by inclusion in the district. Such consent may be indicated by signing a petition for organization or annexation as in this act provided. District assessments, charges, and tolls against said lands shall not be assessed as taxes, but shall be billed to the state land register, who shall voucher the same to the appropriate officer or officers for payment, and such officer or officers are hereby authorized to pay the same out of any state funds not otherwise appropriated. Contracts for the sale of such lands shall be conditioned upon the payment by the purchaser of such assessments, charges and tolls, and upon cancelation of such contracts payments due the district shall be made by the state as above provided.

SEC. 46. Vested interests in or to structures, works and property or water rights owned or used in connection with mining or power development shall never be affected by or taken under the provisions of this act, saving and excepting that rights of way may be acquired by the district over or across such works or property.

SEC. 47. Upon the filing of a petition in the district court setting forth that an irrigation district should be forthwith dissolved, such petition to be signed by at least a majority of the electors owning at least two-thirds of the land in said district, the court shall make its order setting said petition for hearing, giving at least three weeks notice by publication in a newspaper published in the county in which the district was organized; *provided,* that before the order can be entered dissolving the district the directors must show that the district does not owe any money nor that there are any outstanding bonds of the district or other evidence of indebtedness. Upon a proper showing being made, the court shall enter its order dissolving such irrigation district.

SEC. 48. The board of directors of a district may at any time when deemed advisable call a special election and submit to the qualified electors of the district the question whether or not a special assessment shall be levied for the purpose of raising money to be applied to any of the purposes provided in this act. Such election shall be called and the same shall be held and the result thereof determined and declared in all respects in conformity with the provisions of this act in respect to bond elections. The notice shall specify the amount of money proposed to be raised and the purpose for which it is intended to be used, and whether an equal rate of assessment or a special apportionment of benefits is to be made in that relation if either is proposed. At such election the ballots shall contain the words "Assessment —Yes," or "Assessment—No." If two-thirds or more of the votes cast are "Assessment—Yes," the board shall immediately proceed to apportion the benefits, if such apportionment is to be made, and to levy an assessment sufficient to raise the amount voted. The assessment so levied shall be entered in the assessment book or books by the secretary of the board and collected in the same manner as other assessments provided for herein and when received by the treasurer of the district shall be deposited and kept in the construction fund. At such an election there may be submitted the proposition of authorizing the board of directors to levy each year for a stated number of years assessments not exceeding a stated amount per acre for the purpose of providing a fund from which repairs may be made and replacement and extensions of existing works may be constructed and paid for as the necessity for same arises. In such case plans and specifications need not be made in advance—a general description of the contemplated undertaking shall be sufficient. If said proposition be carried by two-thirds of the electors the board shall be authorized to levy such assessment and same shall be collected as are other assessments under this act. Moneys realized from such assessments shall be deposited and kept in the general fund and disbursed by the treasurer in accord with the direction of the board or rules and regulations established by it.

SEC. 49. Any one of the several divisions of a district may provide for the construction of local drains, laterals or other improvements, or the replacement or extension of existing works or structures, the benefits of which are limited to such division, in the following manner: Upon presentation to the board of directors of the district of a petition, signed by a majority of the electors of such division representing at least one-half of the total acreage thereof, describing in a general way the local matters proposed to be undertaken and naming two electors of such division for local directors thereof, the board of directors of the district shall consider such petition at a regular meeting and if it finds that the law has been complied with shall approve the same and appoint the electors named in the petition as members of the local board. One shall hold office until his successor is elected at the next biennial district election and qualifies, and the other until his successor is elected at the second biennial district election after his appointment and qualifies. The terms of such local directors shall be determined by lot and their successors shall be elected for four-year terms at the biennial elections. The said two local directors, with the director of the district from that division, shall constitute the local board of such division, and such board may provide for the local undertakings above named; being hereby authorized for that purpose in so far as applicable to exercise the powers and perform the duties granted to or imposed upon the board of directors of the district in connection with its affairs. Such local board shall thereupon prepare plans and estimates of the local undertakings proposed to be accomplished by such division, stating therein whether the funds therefor are to be raised by a single special assessment or the said board is to be authorized to secure the necessary amounts by way of annual assessments extending over a stated number of years, and not in excess of a stated amount per acre; and if the latter method is to be used a general statement of the purposes for which the money is to be raised may be substituted for more explicit plans and estimates. Such plans and estimates or statement shall be filed with the secretary of the district, accompanied by a request of the local board that an election be called in the division to authorize the proposed special assessment or assessments and the construction of the proposed works; thereupon the secretary of the board shall give notice of the purpose, time and place of such election, naming the polling place, and inspectors and clerks of election suggested by the local board; such notice to be published and election to be held, as near as may be, as provided in this act for an election for special assessments in the district. If such election fail of the required two-thirds vote of the electors of the division, the terms of office of the local directors shall thereupon terminate and the said local board shall be dissolved. If the special assessment or assessments and construction of the proposed works be authorized at such election, the local board shall levy such assessments, or, as the case may be, shall proceed to the levying of annual assessments, and a list of such assessments or the first annual assessment, if to be made that year, shall be delivered to the treasurer of the district and by him entered in the assessment book or books thereof, and such assessment or assessments and the collection thereof shall thereafter take the course of assessments of the district as in this act provided. All of the above-described proceedings relating to the local undertakings of a division, including apportionment of benefits for undertakings authorized by special election, may be confirmed in court as a part of the confirmation proceedings, or upon petition of the board of directors of the division. Each member of the local board of a division shall receive three dollars per day for each day in attending meetings of the board, or while engaged in official business under the order of the board. When the local undertakings above provided for are accomplished and paid for, a showing to that effect shall be made to the board of directors of the district, and upon the approval thereof by such board the terms of office of the local directors shall terminate, and any moneys of such division in the district treasury shall be appropriately credited to the lands of the division in connection with future assessments against such lands.

SEC. 50. At least as often as once a year after the approval of said plans the board of directors shall make a report to the state engineer of the progress of the work of the district and whether or not the plan formulated under the provisions of this act is being successfully carried out, and whether or not in the opinion of the board the funds available will complete the proposed works. Upon receipt of such report by the state engineer, he shall make such suggestions and recommendations to such board of directors as may be necessary to conserve the best interests of the district.

SEC. 51. On or before the first Tuesday of February of each year the board of directors of each irrigation district shall publish in at least one issue of some newspaper published in the county where the office of the district is located a full, true, and correct statement of the financial condition of said district on the first day of that year, giving a statement of all liabilities and assets of the district.

SEC. 52. The board of directors of each irrigation district, or the secretary thereof, shall at any time allow any member of the board of county commissioners, when acting under the order of such board, to have access to all books, records, and vouchers of the district which are in the possession or control of said board of directors or said secretary.

SEC. 53. Water may be supplied by the district, or by a division thereof when a local board of such division is created and authorized, to towns within or in the vicinity of the district, and an appropriate charge made therefor, when such supply can be developed as an incident of or in connection with the works of the district or the local undertakings of a division.

SEC. 54. In addition to the powers with which irrigation districts are or may be vested under the laws of the state, irrigation districts shall have the following powers: To cooperate and contract with the United States under the federal reclamation act of June 17, 1902, and all acts amendatory thereof or supplemental thereto, or any other act of Congress heretofore or hereafter enacted authorizing or permitting such cooperation, and to cooperate and contract with the State of Nevada under any law heretofore or hereafter enacted authorizing or permitting such cooperation, for purposes of construction of works, whether for irrigation or drainage, or both, or for the acquisition, purchase, extension, operation, or maintenance of constructed works, or for a water supply, or for the assumption as principal or guarantor of indebtedness to the United States on account of district lands or for the collection of moneys due the United States as fiscal agents or otherwise.

SEC. 55. The board of directors shall generally perform all such acts as shall be necessary to carry out the enlarged powers in the foregoing section enumerated. Said board may enter into obligations or contracts with the United States for the aforesaid purposes, and may provide therein for the delivery and distribution of water to the lands of such district under the aforesaid acts of Congress and the rules and regulations established thereunder. The contract may provide for the conveyance to the United States as partial consideration for the privileges obtained by the district under said contract of water rights or other property of the district; and in case contract has been or may hereafter be made with the United States as herein provided bonds of the district may be transferred to or deposited with the United States, if so provided by said contract and authorized as hereinafter set forth, at not less than ninety-five per cent of their par value to the amount to be paid by the district to the United States or any part thereof; the interest, or principal, or both, of said bonds to be raised by assessment and levy as hereinafter prescribed and to be regularly paid to the United States and applied as provided in said contract. Bonds transferred to or deposited with the United States may call for the payment of such interest, not exceeding six per cent per annum, may be of such denomination, and may call for the repayment of the principal at such times as may be agreed upon between the board and the secretary of the interior. The contract with the United States may likewise call for the payment of the amount or amounts to be paid by the district to the United States or any part thereof at such times and in such installments and with such interest charges not exceeding the aforesaid rate as may be agreed upon, and for assessment and levy therefor as hereinafter provided, and the obligations of such contracts shall be a prior lien to any subsequent bond issue. Moreover the board may accept on behalf of the district appointment of the district as fiscal agent of the United States, or authorization of the district by the United States to make collection of moneys for or on behalf of the United States in connection with any federal reclamation project, whereupon the district shall be authorized so to act and to assume the duties and liabilities incident to such action, and the said board shall have full power to do any and all things required by the federal statutes now or hereafter enacted in connection therewith, and all things required by the rules and regulations now or that may hereafter be established by any department of the federal government in regard thereto. Districts cooperating with the United States may rent or lease water to private lands, entrymen, or municipalities in the neighborhood of the district in pursuance of contract with the United States.

SEC. 56. Any proposal to enter into a contract with the United States for the repayment of construction moneys, the cost of a water supply, the operation and maintenance of existing works, or the acquisition of property, and to issue bonds if any be proposed, shall be voted upon at an election wherein proceedings shall be had in so far as applicable in the manner provided in the case of the ordinary issuance of district bonds. Notice of the election herein provided for shall contain, in addition to the information required in the case of ordinary bond election, a statement of the maximum amount of money to be payable to the United States for construction purposes, costs of water supply and acquisition of property, exclusive of penalties and interest, together with a general statement of the property, if any, to be conveyed by the district as hereinabove provided. The ballots at such election shall contain a brief statement of the general purpose of said contract and the amount of the obligation to be assumed, as aforesaid, with the words "Contract—Yes," and "Contract —No," or "Contract and bonds—Yes," and "Contract and bonds—No," as the case may be. The board of directors may submit any such contract or proposed contract and bond issue, if any, to the district court of the county wherein is located the office of said board to determine the validity thereof and the authority of the board to enter into such contract, and the authority for and the validity of the issuance and deposit or transfer of said bonds; whereupon the same proceedings shall be had as in the ordinary case of the judicial determination of the validity of the bonds with like effect.

SEC. 57. All water delivered to the district or the right to the use of which is acquired by the district, under any contract with the United States, shall be distributed and apportioned by the district in accordance with the acts of Congress applicable thereto, the rules and regulations of the secretary of the interior thereunder, and the provisions of said contract, and provision may be made in the contract between the district and the United States for the refusal of water service to any or all lands which may become delinquent in the payment of any assessment, toll or charge levied or imposed for the purpose of carrying out any contract between the district and the United States. In case of contract with the United States under which the district assumes the operation and maintenance of the existing works, assessments, tolls and charges may be levied or imposed by the board of directors, as provided in this act to raise the sums required annually therefor, including amounts due the United States under said contract.

SEC. 58. Any rights of way or other property owned or acquired by the district may be conveyed by the board to the United States in so far as the same may be needed for the construction, operation and maintenance of works by the United States pursuant to this act.

SEC. 59. All payments due or to become due to the United States under any contract between the district and the United States, including such payments of interest and principal on bonds as may be required in connection with a deposit or transfer thereof to the United States, shall be paid, unless otherwise provided by contract, by revenue derived from annual assessments, apportioned as hereinafter prescribed, and levies thereof upon such real property within the district as may be accessible for district purposes under the laws of the state or by tolls and charges as the case may be, and such real property shall be and remain liable to be assessed and levied upon for such payments as herein provided. It shall be the duty of the board of directors annually to levy an assessment, or to impose and cause to be collected tolls or charges sufficient to raise the money necessary to meet all payments when due as provided in the contract. All moneys collected in pursuance of such contract by assessment and levies or otherwise, and to be paid to the United States, shall be paid into the district treasury and held in a fund to be known as the "United States Contract Fund," to be used for payments due to the United States under any such contract. Public lands of the United States within any district shall be subject to assessment for all purposes of this act to the extent provided for by the act of Congress approved August 11, 1916, entitled "An act to promote reclamation of arid lands," or any other law which may hereafter be enacted by Congress in the same relation, upon full compliance therewith by the district. Nothing in this act contained shall be construed to relieve the district from obligation to pay as a district in case of default of any land, unless so provided by the said contract between the district and the United States.

SEC. 60. The board may also provide by contract with the United States for the release of mortgages or liens given or reserved to the United States upon district lands, and may provide for the assumption by the district, either as principal or guarantor, of indebtedness to the United States on account of district lands, and apportion to each tract of land so released, benefits in the amount of the obligations to the United States so provided to be released; and the contract between the district and the United States may provide for the collection and payment of indebtedness so incurred or assumed by the district and the tax or assessment for the same at the same times and in the same amounts or installments provided in the federal reclamation laws, and if so provided in the contract, such taxes and assessments shall become delinquent at the same dates provided in the act of Congress of August 13, 1914 (38 Stats. 686), known as the reclamation extension act, and in that event, if it be provided in the contract that the United States waives any penalties for delinquency other or greater than those named in the said act of Congress of August 13, 1914, then, instead of the penalties otherwise provided in state laws, the penalties for delinquency in the payment of that part of the tax representing the special assessment for payment of the obligations of the district to the United States shall be the penalties named in the said act of Congress of August 13, 1914, and the amount required to be paid in case of any redemption from any tax sale or tax judgment shall be determined by figuring the part thereof due to the United States upon the basis of the amount of such special assessment levied for the purpose of paying the United States plus the penalties named in said act of Congress of August 13, 1914. And the said board shall have full power to do any and all things required by the federal statutes now or hereafter enacted in connection therewith, and all things required by the rules and regulations now or that may hereafter be established by any department of the federal government in regard thereto.

SEC. 61. The assessment required in any year to meet the payment due to the. United States under the contract as in this act provided may be in accord with an apportionment of benefits made in or in pursuance of such contract and in the ascertainment of such benefits there shall be taken into account the provisions of the contract between the United States and the district, the federal laws applicable thereto, and the notice and regulations issued in pursuance of said laws, and in case such contract is for the assumption by the district as principal or guarantor of indebtedness to the United States theretofore existing on account of district lands, there shall be further taken into account the provision of existing contracts carrying such indebtedness and the amounts of such liens as may be released in pursuance of the contract between the United States and the district.

SEC. 62. Where contract shall have been entered into and is in force and effect between the United States and any irrigation district the district shall not be dissolved, nor shall the boundaries be changed, except upon written consent of the secretary of the interior, filed with the official records of the district. If such consent be given and lands be excluded, the areas excluded shall be free from all liens and charges for payments to become due to the United States. The board of directors of a district is hereby relieved from the duties imposed upon it in sections 15 and 30 of this act in so far as the same may not be required in case of contract between the district and the United States, and in that relation may take advantage of or adopt such surveys and plans as may have been or be made by the United States.

SEC. 63. When an irrigation district comprises lands which are served by works constructed by the United States and the portion of such works situated in a division of the district may be regarded as a separate unit of the larger system for operation and maintenance purposes, or when local drains, laterals, or other improvements may be provided as additions to such works and constitute benefits limited to such division, or when the replacement or extension of such works or some part thereof would constitute benefits limited to such division, a petition signed by the requisite number of electors of such division may be presented to the board of directors of the district and a local board of directors of such division created as provided in this act; whereupon such board of directors shall have the power to contract with the United States for the operation of the existing system aforesaid, or for the construction either by such division or by the United States of local drains, laterals or other improvements and for the operation and maintenance thereof, or for the replacement or extension of existing works or structures and for the operation and maintenance thereof or any separate part of the same; *provided,* that such contract shall first be authorized by a special election held for the purpose in such division and for the purpose of authorizing the local board of directors to levy an assessment or assessments, as provided in this act, to secure the moneys required to carry out said contract, including the amounts that will be due the United States thereunder and that will be required for the construction of the proposed local drains, laterals, or other improvements, or for the replacement and extension of existing works or structures. Where it is proposed that a division shall assume only the operation and maintenance of existing works an election shall be held upon the contract in the same manner, but the local board of directors, after said contract is made in pursuance of the authority granted in such election, shall have the power to levy assessments or impose tolls and charges annually or otherwise to raise the amounts necessary to carry out said contract and to operate and maintain said works, including amounts to be paid to the United States under said contract, in the same manner and to the same effect as can be done by the board of directors of the district under the provisions of this act. Where local drains, laterals or improvements are to be constructed, or existing works or structures replaced or extended, and are thereafter to be operated and maintained by the division, the local board shall have similar power to levy assessments and to impose tolls or charges to raise the money required for such operation and maintenance, including amounts due the United States in that relation. The works described in the contract with the United States shall be constructed, replaced or extended by such local board of directors, and the money raised by such special assessment therefor or for the operation and maintenance thereof shall be collected, kept and disbursed, and the apportionment of benefits made, as in this act provided when a division of the district is authorized to provide for local undertakings, the benefits of which are limited to such division; *provided*, that the provisions of this act relating to cooperation between a district and the United States, including those relating to the distribution and apportionment of water and the apportionment of benefits, shall apply in case of contract between the United States and a division of a district in so far as applicable. The execution of such contract with the United States and all proceedings ancillary thereto may be confirmed in court as a part of the confirmation proceedings instituted by the district, or upon petition by the board of directors of the division.

SEC. 64. When an irrigation district comprises lands which are or may be served by works constructed by the United States, and a contract is proposed to be entered into with the United States for the operation and maintenance by the district of the existing works, or for the construction of a drainage system or other extension or improvement of such works, and the lands in a division of the district may be regarded as clearly outside the scope of such contract, the election thereon and for the authorization of the program or undertaking contemplated thereby may be confined to the remaining portion of the district exclusive of such division, and the apportionment of the benefits may be made accordingly; otherwise the proceedings in connection with such contract and the program or undertaking contemplated thereby shall be as heretofore provided in this act.

SEC. 65. In any case where an irrigation district is appointed fiscal agent of the United States in connection with any federal reclamation project, or by the United States, or under contract therewith, is authorized or required to make collection of moneys on behalf of the United States, or for payments due the United States under any such contract, each director of the district, and the secretary and the treasurer thereof, shall execute a further and additional bond in such sum as the secretary of the interior may require, conditioned for the faithful discharge of the duties of his office, or as fiscal or other agent of the United States, or both; and any such bonds may be sued upon by the United States or any person injured by the failure of such officer or officers of the district to fully, promptly or completely perform their respective duties. This requirement shall apply to the directors of a division, and in so far as applicable to the officers of a district acting in that relation, in case of contract between the United States and such division. In all cases of contracts with the United States as above described the board of directors of the district, or of a division thereof, and the secretary and treasurer of a district, shall at any time allow any officer or employee of the United States, when acting under the order of the secretary of the interior, to have access to all books, records and documents which are in the possession or control of such officers.

SEC. 66. Whenever in this act any notice is required to be given by publication, such provision shall be satisfied by publishing the same in a weekly newspaper the same number of times consecutively as the number of weeks mentioned in the requirement.

SEC. 67. Whenever the words "irrigation district," or "district" are used in this act, they shall be held to mean any irrigation district heretofore organized under the laws of the state as well as under this act, to the full extent required to accomplish the purposes of this act; and whenever the words "county treasurer" or "treasurer of the county" are used in this act, they shall as well be held to mean "ex officio tax receiver" or "tax receiver" of the county.

SEC. 68. Nothing in this act shall be so construed as to affect the validity of any district heretofore organized under the laws of this state, or its rights in or to property, or any of its rights or privileges of whatsoever kind or nature; but said districts are hereby made subject to the provisions of this act as far as applicable; nor shall it affect, impair, or discharge any contract, obligation, lien or charge for, or upon which it was or might become liable or chargeable had not this act been passed; nor shall it affect the validity of any bonds which have been issued but not sold, nor shall it affect any action which now may be pending. In such districts as have been heretofore organized, and in which directors of the various divisions thereof have been elected by the votes of the electors of the district at large, such elections are hereby confirmed.

SEC. 69. Nothing in this act shall be construed as repealing or in any wise modifying the provisions of any other act relating to the subject of irrigation or drainage except such as may be contained in the act entitled "An act to provide for the organization and government of drainage, irrigation and water storage districts, to provide for the acquisition of water and other property, and for the distribution of the water thereby for irrigation purposes, and for other matters properly connected therewith," approved March 20, 1911, and subsequent acts supplementary thereto or amendatory thereof, all of which acts, so far as they may be inconsistent herewith, are hereby repealed.

SEC. 70. This act may be referred to in any action, proceeding or legislative enactment as "The Nevada Irrigation District Act," and whenever the words "irrigation district" are or have been used in any action or proceeding or in any act or resolution of the legislature such words shall be construed to mean an irrigation district organized under the provisions of the act approved March 20, 1911, or acts supplementary thereto or amendatory thereof, referred to in the preceding section, or an irrigation district organized or existing under this act.